# Me, Too, Zacchaeus

## Conversations
## With
## the Man
## in the Tree
## and Other
## Bible
## Personalities

### Betty Westrom Skold

Illustrated by
Carol Skold Uecker

**PORCH LIGHT Press**

*Me Too, Zacchaeus*
*Conversations With the Man in the Tree*
*and Other Bible Personalities*

Copyright © 1995 by Betty Westrom Skold

Illustrated by Carol Skold Uecker

Book design by Cherene Bebeau

(Scripture quotations are) from the *Revised Standard Version of the Bible,* copyright 1946, 1952, 1971, by the Division of Christian Education of the National Council of the Churches of Christ in the USA. Used by permission.

Library of Congress Catalog Card No. 95–67099

International Standard Book Number:    0-9645240-0-7

Printed by Fairway Foods
Printed in the United States of America.

*This book is dedicated to*

*my good friend Eric Gustavson,*

*who walks easily in the company*

*of Bible personalities and*

*shares with them a whole set*

*of lively adventures---*

*his own and theirs.*

# Contents

# Preface

How often, as you read the Bible, do you nod knowingly and say under your breath, "I know the feeling"?  Again and again I am startled to find myself mirrored in the lives of these personalities who lived 20 or more centuries ago.

We believe in the Incarnation, that God himself became a human being.  For a few years, during that historic visit, Jesus of Nazareth walked in the shoes of humankind.  Isn't it a good pattern for us, too, in our dealings with each other?

We can be more forgiving with the short–tempered man at the office by reminding ourselves that we, too, have lashed out with words we'd like to take back.  We can be understanding toward the nosey woman next door if we put ourselves in her place, asking ourselves how well we might handle the bleakness of living alone.  Why not do that with Bible personalities as well?

We can believe the Bible precisely because its characters are so real.  Nobody could have made them up.  We sense their authenticity.  If we had been building a religion, we would have put together a whole cast of heroic super–persons and would have been bored to death by those one–dimensional characters.

But somehow we can be interested in David because he cheats as much as he inspires.  He connives, he despairs, he is overwhelmed by lust.  David, with all his flaws, attains greatness because he takes God seriously.  He learns the agonizing necessity for repentance.

The free verse reflections in this book invite you to find yourself in the pages of the Bible, to identify with each of the characters. If you fantasize what it would be like to be Jeremiah or Elizabeth or Noah, you may learn more about them, and more about yourself, too. If you read Bible stories with some creative imagination, they will come alive for you. These characters are not stiff little drawings from Sunday school books. They are passionate personalities with a timeless set of emotions and attitudes.

I'd like to think I'm not just a latter–day ventriloquist putting words into their mouths posthumously. I dare to hope that, if I were to share may fears with them, my anxieties and my frustrations, that Mary Magdalene and Zacchaeus and the Woman at the Well would nod knowingly and murmur the First Century equivalent of "Join the club."

The book is meant just to get you started. There's no reason why you can't take it from there and enjoy some imaginary conversations of your own.

This book has given me special pleasure, since my daughter, Carol Skold Uecker, is its illustrator. For many years we have collaborated on the Family Christmas card, but this marks the first time we have pooled our creative gifts in a book.

For their helpful suggestions in the preparation of the manuscript, I am grateful to my husband, Bill Skold, my daughter, Carol Uecker, and to seven readers: Maxine Jenkins, Wesley Lindstrom, Violet Towley, Mim Haug, Rita Wigfield, Wayne Hoganson, and Linda Zdrazil.

I also want to thank Tom Heie for his encouragement and wise counsel in bringing this book to publication.

# Me, Too, Zacchaeus

*Conversations
With
the Man
in the Tree
and Other
Bible
Personalities*

# Me, Too, Zacchaeus

*And there was a man named Zacchaeus; he was a chief tax collector, and rich. And he sought to see who Jesus was, but could not, on account of the crowd, because he was small of stature. So he ran on ahead and climbed up into a sycamore tree to see him, for he was to pass that way. And when Jesus came to the place, he looked up and said to him, Zacchaeus, make haste and come down; for I must stay at your house today. Luke 19: 2–5.*

I'm like you, Zacchaeus.
Don't laugh. I mean it.
I'm not rich, of course,
and tree–climbing is not my style.
To me, even the bottom branch looks risky.

How could I be like you?
There you were, shinnying up a tree
like some lively nine–year old.

Well, the way I see it, Zacchaeus,
a nine–year old boy
climbs trees for one of two reasons---
he wants to see
or he wants to be seen.

Up there
nobody else can block his view.
Up there
he's as tall as anybody.

and if he is discovered,
he grins in triumph,
"Look what I dare do!"

You climbed the tree
in order to see, Zacchaeus.
You wanted a better view,
to see for yourself
this Jesus you'd heard about.

*Being* seen
was the last thing you needed.

If the others bothered to look up,
they probably said,
"Now what is he up to—
Zacchaeus,
that loner, that runt,
that crook?"

They knew what you were.
They didn't like
your way of doing business.

You climbed the tree
to see, Zacchaeus.
You were looking for something
to fill that empty space
in your life.

You wanted to see,

but you were seen by him,
not as a squat, pathetic little man,
clinging to a tree limb,
but as a dinner companion,
a person worth knowing,
a potential friend.

You wanted a clearer view.
Me, too, Zacchaeus.
I need to see him for myself.
I stretch to see more clearly.

As I said before,
I'd feel ridiculous, climbing trees,
but tree climbing
is not the point.

Wherever I hide myself,
he spots me,
sees my possibilities.

My looking for God
is less important...
far less important...
than his looking for me.

# Committee of One

*The house which King Solomon built for the Lord was sixty cubits long, twenty cubits wide, and thirty cubits high.  I Kings, 6: 2*

You had it right, Solomon.
(or is it "Your Majesty"?)
Lucky for your temple project
that it happened
back the In B.B.C.
(Before Building Committees).

If you had waited
for a  few centuries,
a committee of 15
would have had to decide.
Fifteen people,
fifteen different ideas
of what a temple should be.

Slaughterhouse?
Concert hall?
Dwelling place
of the Most High?
All of the above---
and that gets complicated.

Fifteen people arguing
that 60 cubits was too long
or too short,

that 20 cubits was too wide--
or too narrow.

Oh, sure,
you managed 30,000 timber workers,
20,000 burden bearers,
80,000 stone cutters.
No picnic,
but no problem.

You were still in full charge
of the basic vision,
a committee of one.
God wanted it built,
and the details were up to you.
You didn't have to clear it
with anybody.

If you got carried away
with the gold and silver touches,
nobody threatened
to cancel his pledge.

Our building project?
Well, it's modest
by your standards,
but for 15 people
it's agony.

Altar in the middle?
Baptismal font in back?
How much storage?

What color carpeting?
Which stained glass design?

Committee of one
or committee of fifteen,
the basic question is the same.
"What indestructible thing
will this temple contain?"

From your life, Solomon,
from the history of your people,
we have learned,
our treasure
is that which we can carry away
from a temple
that lies in ruins.

# About Hiding Places

*And they heard the sound of the Lord God walking in the
garden in the cool of the day, and the man and his wife
hid themselves from the presence of the Lord God
among the trees of the garden. But the Lord God called
to the man, and said to him, "Where are you" and he
said, "I heard the sound of thee in the garden, and I was
afraid, because I was naked; and I hid myself."
Genesis 3: 8–10*

It was fear
that sent you there,
wasn't it, Adam?

You went to your hiding place
because you has disobeyed...
and because God knew...
and because you knew that God knew.

Guilt and fear sent you
to your hiding place.

When I go to a hiding place,
driven by guilt or fear,
I remember hiding games
from my childhood.

And I remember
how I couldn't quite decide
whether I did or didn't
want to get caught.

Sometimes the place
was behind a tree,
sometimes under a stairway
or in a dark closet.

But I have noticed one thing
about hiding places.
They're not much good
for anything else.

# I Need Roots

*Now the Lord said to Abram, "Go from your country and your kindred and your father's house to the land that I will show you, and I will make of you a great nation, and I will bless you, and make your name great, so that you will be a blessing. I will bless those who bless you, and him who curses you I will curse; and by you all the families of the earth shall bless themselves. So Abram went, as the Lord had told him; and Lot went with him. Abram was seventy–five years old when he departed from Haran. Genesis 12: 1–4.*

I'm your basic homebody, Abraham.
I need roots.
It wouldn't enter my mind
to just pick up
and move somewhere else.

I feel at home here.
Even talk of a Promised Land
would never be enough
to shake me loose.

I have to hand it to you, Abraham.
At your age
it would have been a  lot easier
to just stay put.

You were successful,
respected,
settled.

If the rocking chair
had been invented,
you had earned the right
to relax in it.

Nothing wrong with God's promises---
You'd find a homeland.
You'd be a father at last,
a father of nations.

But trumpet calls
are for the young.

You had a thousand and one reasons
to beg off.
"I love you , Lord,
but no, thanks.
Don't ask me to do that.
I'm old.  I'm a little tired,
and I'd like to stay put."

But against all evidence
you believed.
You followed wherever the promises led,
kept going until they came true.

Roots were not your God, Abraham,
and that made all the difference.

Through your obedience
we all have roots.
We are all rooted in the promises of God.

# Your Best Gift

*For this child I prayed; and the Lord has granted me my
petition which I made to him. Therefore I have lent him
to the Lord; as long as he lives, he is lent to the Lord."
And they worshiped the Lord there. I Samuel I: 27 & 28.*

You did a fine thing, Hannah.
I mean that.

You gave your son Samuel
to God's work
for all the right reasons.

You didn't just drop him off
at the temple
for your own convenience,
because it simplified your life,
because you knew he's be in good hands.

It wasn't just
a grand gesture,
a display of piety
for the benefit
of the neighbors.

You did it
because you loved God
and because Samuel
was the best gift
you had to give.

After all that waiting,
after all those barren years,
years of humiliation,
you had a child to hold,
and you gave him back to God.

I admire you, Hannah,
but for me
it just wouldn't wash...
not in America,
not in this century.

We can love our kids.
We can feed them
and chauffeur them
and referee their arguments,
but they do their own deciding.

At the font, we make promises for them.
At confirmation they speak their own,
but we feel powerless before everything
that threatens those words of promise.

They do their own deciding.
It's right that they should,
but it isn't easy.
I can't handle it, Hannah.

It's their decision,
but I wince at the words,
"Don't wake me for church.
I'm sleeping in."

# What Kept You Going. Noah?

*And God said to Noah, "I have been determined to make
an end of all flesh; for the earth is filled with violence
through them; behold, I will destroy them with the
earth. Make yourself an ark of gopher wood; make
rooms in the ark, and cover it inside and out with pitch.
This is how you are to make it; the length of the ark
three hundred cubits, its breadth fifty cubits, and its
height thirty cubits." Genesis 6: 13–15*

As one "do–it–yourselfer" to another, Noah,
didn't you ever feel
like chucking it?

Oh, God's instructions were helpful enough,
but you were still the one
who had to keep on building.

You were the guy who had to deal
with neighbors
who shook their heads
and walked away, laughing.

After a day of nail–pounding,
did you ever mutter to yourself,
"I still don't think
it looks like rain"?

At that point,
before the skies opened,

it might have helped
if God had given some solid sign,
some proof
that He meant business.

After it was over,
He hung a rainbow
for all the world to see,
His sign that said, "Never again."

But there you were, Noah,
not even a mutter of thunder,
and there you were
building that enormous ark,
rounding up all those animals...
with no guarantees!

As it turned out,
the rains did come.
Your arkful did survive,
but how could you know, Noah?

How could you know that danger was real?
How could you know
that God's blueprints
held the answer?

How can *I* know?

## I Envy You, Jacob

*And he came to a certain place, and stayed there that*
*night, because the sun had set. Taking one of the stones*
*of the place, he put it under his head and lay down in that*
*place to sleep. And he dreamed that there was a ladder*
*set up on the earth, and the top of it reached to heaven;*
*and behold, the angels of God were ascending and*
*descending on it! and behold, the Lord stood above it*
*and said, "I am the Lord, the God of Abraham your father*
*and the God of Isaac; the land on which you lie I will*
*give to you and your descendants." Genesis, 28: 11–13.*

Sometimes I'm envious
of your vision, Jacob.
God went out of his way
to make things clear to you.

There was God's message
in one spectacular skyful.
There was the staircase to heaven.
There were the angels,
moving up and down.

But of course
that isn't the whole story, is it?
You vision didn't come to you
in some comfortable valley, did it?
It came on a barren hilltop.

If God has a vision for me,

I may have to climb, too, Jacob.
I may have to explore some high, stark,
moonscape of experience.

To catch my vision,
I may have to lay my head
on a pillow of stone.

# *Manna Again?*

*Now the rabble that was among them had a strong*
*craving; and the people of Israel also wept again, and*
*said, "Oh, that we had meat to eat! We remember the*
*fish we ate in Egypt for nothing, the cucumbers, the*
*melons, the leeks, the onions, and the garlic; but now*
*our strength is dried up, and there is nothing at all but*
*this manna to look at." Numbers, 11: 4–6.*

I couldn't count the times it happened,
the times I sighed over leftovers
because someone took a notion
they were tired of meat loaf
or buttered carrots
or scrambled eggs.

But there you all were
in the wilderness, Moses,
cut off from everything,
threatened by starvation,
and God fed you with a miracle.

Did they actually say it, Moses?
Did they really grumble,
"Manna again?"
They did.
They seemed to be chronic complainers;
and on a daily basis, even a miracle gets tedious.

After 40 years,
even a manna windfall
tastes a little flat.

When I begin to take daily miracles for granted,
when my gratitude wears thin,
I'll be thinking about all of you, Moses.
O.K.?

# *Your Pictures Don't Do You Justice*

*And while they were there, the time came for her to be
delivered and she gave birth to her first–born son and
wrapped him in swaddling cloths, and laid him in a
manger, because there was no place for them in the inn.
Luke 2: 6–7.*

Mary, your pictures don't do you justice.
You weren't like
the Madonna of the art galleries.

You were younger when your baby came,
and more shy,
and the clothes you wore
were plain and rough.

I know you loved him, Mary,
how you loved the child he was
and worshipped the Savior he became.

For you, his birth was mystery
and joy.

Every mother...every father, too...
has felt something like it...
mystery,
joy.

Any parent feels awe
for beauty and innocence,
though we dare not call that worship.

We wrap them close
in childhood's blankets,
shielding them from cold winds,
protecting them,
fearful of that world
that lies waiting
to hurt them.

We give them
band–aids
and umbrellas
and snow boots.

We equip them
with shatter–proof lenses
and suntan lotion,
because there is no way
we can protect them
from other hurts.
We guard them
from surface dangers
because there are deeper dangers
we cannot even name.

They shrug off
the fragile armor
that we throw over them,
and walk out of sight.
If they have fears,
they do not show.

The angel messenger
had given you an advantage, Mary.
From the beginning
your son was special.
You had some sense
of his power.

But when you unwrapped his swaddling clothes
for the last time,
was there no grief?

How could you trust his goodness
to a world of evil?
How could you be sure
his innocence
would remain unflawed?

You let him grow up, Mary.
How did you dare?

# Giants Make Me Nervous

*And when the Philistine looked, and saw David, he
disdained him; for he was but a youth, ruddy and comely
in appearance... The Philistine said to David, "Come to
me, and I will give your flesh to the birds of the air and
to the beasts of the field." Then David said to the
Philistine, "You come to me with a sword and with a
spear and with a javelin; but I come to you in the name
of the Lord of hosts, the God of the armies of Israel,
whom you have defied. I Samuel 17:42, 44–46.*

Maybe it's because I'm a lot older
than you were, David,
but I would have folded.
Giants make me nervous.

Sometimes I seem to meet
nothing but Goliaths,
bold, confident people
who make me feel small.

I feel threatened by them.
I look around.
I grope for weapons.

Of course it wasn't really
the rock and the sling
that did it for you,
was it, David?

I mean, the weapon is never the point.
Faith and trust and obedience
were the equipment
that made the real difference.
Right?

Faith...trust...obedience...
My equipment, too,
when giants make me nervous.

# The Neighbor Boy

*And when they had performed everything according to*
*the law of the lord, they returned to Galilee, to their own*
*city, Nazareth. And the child grew and became strong,*
*filled with wisdom; and the favor of God was upon him.*
*Luke 2: 39–40.*

Nazareth neighbors,
how did you see him?

We focus
on the glowing account of his birth,
the high drama
of the crucifixion,
the electrifying news
of the resurrection.

But tell me
about the unchronicled years,
those years of marking time
in your little town,
that sleepy town,
where everybody knew his name.
Is there something I should know
about those years
when he was involved
with the ordinary?

How did he fit in?
Did he pick a basket of olives,

crush a few grapes,
fish from the lake,
sweep up sawdust and shavings
in the carpenter shop?

Did he hike alone
in the Galilean hills?
Did he help his mother
carry water jars to the well?

At Passover time
did he ask the ancient questions?
Did he greet you on the street
and play at games
with your children?

What can I learn
for my own time of commonplace routine?

I can handle crises just fine,
but humdrum makes me restless.
Something in me
wants sparks to fly.

Remind me about that neighbor boy,
obedient to his parents,
that boy who, without fanfare,
grew in wisdom and in stature
and in favor with God and man.

# *Torch–passing Isn't Easy*

*You yourselves bear me witness, that I said, I am not the*
*Christ, but I have been sent before him.  He must in-*
*crease, but I must decrease.  John 3:  28, 30.*

You're John, aren't you?
John the Baptist?

I have a confession to make.
Torch–passing doesn't come
naturally to me.
I'm not too good
at bowing out.

I admire the way
you handled it, John.
Your timing
was just about perfect.

You had had quite a following
of your own.
When you spoke, people listened.
When you  baptized, people came.

But then the time came,
the right time to bow out.
The main event was waiting in the wings,
and your big voice boomed,
"He must increase.  I must decrease."
I'm having a hard time learning that, John.

Teach me.

Teach me that,
when the time is right,
stepping aside is not a weak move.

When I look at my child grown tall,
I need  the good sense to say,
"He must increase.
I must decrease."

When younger leaders
stand ready to take over
my job at church,
show me how to step back
from center stage.
"They must increase.
I must decrease."

When my life gets cluttered
with too many projects,
too many promises,
shout it in my ear, John,
"Prepare ye the way of the Lord!"

Give me your sense of timing.
"He must increase.
I must decrease."

# The Wilderness Wasn't All Bad

*And the Lord went before them by day in a pillar of*
*cloud to lead them along the way, and by night in a*
*pillar of fire to give them light, that they might travel*
*by day and by  night.  Exodus 13: 21.*

The Wilderness
wasn't all bad,
was it Moses?

You all stuck together
because you had to,
and you got into the habit
of looking up.

You kept one eye on that pillar of cloud
or the pillar of fire,
because without God
it was hopeless.

Later, in the Promised Land,
the others might even remember them
as "the Good Old Days,"
days when they needed each other
and they knew it.

I know the feeling, Moses.
I look back on our family's "hard times,"
remembering the aging car
and the creamed dried beef

and the skimpy allowances,
remembering how we had to save up
for birthdays,
and how we popped our own corn
for the drive–in movie.

But God was our pillar of cloud
and our pillar of fire,
and we had time for each other.

I don't want to forget that time, Moses.
I don't want to grow away
from our "wilderness experience."

# Did She Wear Out Her Welcome?

*In those days Mary arose and went with haste into the*
*hill country, to a city of Judah, and she entered the*
*house of Zechariah and greeted Elizabeth. And when*
*Elizabeth heard the greeting of Mary, the babe leaped in*
*her womb; and Elizabeth was filled with the Holy Spirit*
*and she exclaimed with a loud cry, "Blessed are you*
*among women, and blessed is the fruit of your*
*womb."...and Mary remained with her about three*
*months, and returned to her home. Luke 1: 39–41 & 56.*

The truth, Elizabeth---
did she or didn't she
wear out her welcome?

I like company, too,
for short visits,
but three months:
Your cousin Mary came
and she stayed for three months.

I'd say
that was a little much.

You should see my calendar, Elizabeth.
Commitments...
to me they're important commitments.

I mean my schedule
just couldn't handle that.

I'd have other things to do
than sitting around
talking about babies.

I enjoy friends, Elizabeth.
I have cousins, too,
all busy,
all committed to things.

Some day
maybe we'll have time
for each other.

Some day things will settle down.
Some day.....

# *His Workmanship*

*And the child grew and became strong, filled with
wisdom; and the favor of God was upon him. Luke 2: 40.
For we are his workmanship, created in Christ Jesus for
good works, which God prepared beforehand, that we
should walk in them. Ephesians 2: 10.*

You taught him workmanship, Joseph.
You showed him the importance
of driving nails straight, of measuring carefully,
of smoothing rough edges.

The boy had a quick mind,
good hands.
Good help around the shop,
I'm sure.

But if Jesus was both God and man,
then the boy Jesus
was both God and child.
What did that mean?

As human father
you taught that boy workmanship,
but on a deeper level
weren't your own skills
a gift from him?
Weren't you carpenter's hands
a product
of his workmanship?

# The Tree in the Garden

*And the woman said to the serpent, "We may eat of the fruit of the trees of the garden; but God said, 'You shall not eat of the fruit of the tree which is in the midst of the garden, neither shall you touch it, lest you die.'" But the serpent said to the woman, "You will not die. For God knows that when you eat of it your eyes will be opened, and you will be like God, knowing good and evil." So when the woman saw that the tree was good for food, and that it was a delight to the eyes, and that the tree was to be desired to make one wise, she took of its fruit and ate; and she also gave some to her husband, and he ate. Genesis 3: 2–6.*

When you helped yourself to the fruit, Eve,
did you stop to think?
It was the snakes's word against God's,
wasn't it?
The snake's promise of wisdom
seemed to cancel out God's warning.
Maybe you even found excuses of your own.

Maybe you reasoned,
"The tree is heavy with apples.
They'll never be missed."
Or maybe you said,
"We're alone in the Garden.
Who else would go hungry?"

Only one tree was forbidden. Why?

The one tree—one act forbidden—
Was it  God's towering reminder,
"I am in charge of the Garden!"?

That one restriction...
the point at which
God's "Thou shalt not"
met your "Why not?"

You reached for the fruit,
shared it with Adam,
and from that moment on
you reached in pain.

I reach too, Eve.
We all do.
The one forbidden tree goads us
with its "Why Not?"

Do we have a petty God?
A vindictive God?
Does God enjoy saying, "Don't touch"?
The answer is "No."

But God is still in charge
of the garden.

We reach,
we bite the fruit,
then we stand in a bramble patch,
remembering Eden.

*Now when Jesus was born in Bethlehem of Judea in the days of Herod the king, behold, wise men from the East came to Jerusalem, saying, "Where is he who has been born king of the Jews? For we have seen his star in the East, and have come to worship him." Matthew 2: 1,2.*

Wisemen,
could we talk?
I have something to say to you,
yes, all of you.

I made the journey, too.
I went to Bethlehem
mostly because of what
I had read.

I went
remembering that picture
in my old
Sunday school papers---
three bearded men,
three camels,
one blinding star.

Like you,
I went to see for myself.
I went to Bethlehem, too,
but I chose a handy date,
a good time of year,
March,

when I was sick
of Minnesota winter
and things were slow
at work.

You couldn't say
I just dropped everything
and took off.

But you puzzle me, Wisemen---
three intellectuals,
carrying little gifts,
hurrying off
to a baby shower.

Soft–eyed animals,
tall Joseph,
gentle mother,
sleeping baby--
did they surprise you?

If you had asked questions,
I'd have understood.
Questions had always been
your stock in trade.

But what happened?
What was there
about that manger that erased every question?

What happened?
You fell down
and worshiped.

# *Now Where Have You Been?*

*After three days they found him in the temple, sitting
among the teachers, listening to them and asking them
questions; and all who heard him were amazed at his
understanding and his answers. And when they saw him
they were astonished; and his mother said to him, "Son,
why have you treated us so? Behold, your father and I
have been looking for you anxiously." Luke 2: 46–48.*

There's always an explanation,
isn't there, Mary,
(when the boy finally shows up
and you know he's safe)?

A mother feels relief, of course,
but it can't erase
all those other feelings.

When the panic drains away,
a mother still feels hurt and anger.
She still asks the question,
"How could you do this to me?"
She still strains to find meanings
in non–replies.

Jesus was just twelve,
and I, for one, think you had a right to say,
"Your father and I have sought thee sorrowing."
Not too different from my own words,
"You should have known we'd worry."

or "At least you could have phoned."

He was teaching in the temple,
beginning to do his real job.
Were you expected to know that?

But every growing person
yanks at the umbilical cord.
Every child has pressing business
away from family.

Every child discovers
things more important
than showing up for dinner.

# How Could You Be So Picky?

*The Pharisee stood and prayed thus with himself, "God, I thank thee that I am not like other men, extortioners, unjust, adulterers, or even like this tax collector. I fast twice a week, I give tithes of all that I get." Luke 18: 11–12*

It's easy to find fault with you, Pharisees.
We laugh at your picky regulations.
Couldn't you see
how silly they had become?
It seems so obvious.

Did you need that tangle
of Mickey Mouse rules?
Why all that fuss
about eating fat
and picking grain on the Sabbath
and reporting mildew to the priest?

Whose business was it
if someone wanted
to hitch an ox and donkey together
for plowing?

But how about my own "Little Commandments,"
the code handed down
from my mother?
How about my clutter
of little rules?

"Don't run upstairs
with scissors in your hand."

"Don't hold the refrigerator door open,
taking inventory."

"Don't dunk your toast in the grape juice,
or lick your finger to turn pages,
or use a toothpick at the table."

Like Old Testament legalists,
we supplement the great Commandments
with a swarm of small ones.

We cling to the picky rules
and neglect those that count.
Only the Lord can help us
to simplify.

Only he can take us
back to the basics:
"Love your God."
"Love your neighbor."

# Don't Be Too Hard on Them, Joseph

*Now Israel loved Joseph more than any other of his*
*children, because he was the son of his old age; and he*
*made him a long robe with sleeves. But when his*
*brothers saw that their father loved him more than all*
*his brothers, they hated him, and could not speak*
*peaceably to him...They saw him afar off, and before he*
*came near to them they conspired against him to kill*
*him. They said to one another, "Here comes this*
*dreamer. Come now, let us kill him and throw him into*
*one of the pits; then we shall say that a wild beast has*
*devoured him, and we shall see what will become of his*
*dreams." Genesis 37: 3,4, 18–20.*

Don't be too hard
on your brothers, Joseph.

It was a handsome coat,
and it really didn't seem fair.

Did you or didn't you
strut a little,
showing off your coat
of many colors?

In their eyes
you had always been a braggart,
a tattletale,
and now you had been singled out,
given something special.

It rubbed your brothers the wrong way.
It doesn't make it right,
but they were made cold by envy,
so they ganged up on you,
pooled their anger.
Who wouldn't?

It was their only way
of striking back
against a father
who hadn't played fair.

It hurt you.
It hurt your father,
and they wanted it to hurt.

Think about it, Joseph.
What if the coat had gone
to Reuben
or to Asher
or to Levi?

And what if he
had worn it
a little too proudly?

# Show Me Resurrection

*Martha said to Jesus, "Lord, if you had been here, my brother would not have died. And even now I know that whatever you ask from God, God will give you." Jesus said to her, "Your brother will rise again." Martha said to him, "I know that he will rise again in the resurrection at the last day." Jesus said to her, "I am the resurrection and the life; he who believes in me, though he die, yet shall he live." John 11: 21–25.*

Martha,
I am beginning to learn
how you felt,
how something in you died
with the death of Lazarus.

Tears burn my own cheek.
Now I begin to understand.
Only your brother was buried.
You couldn't bury your sorrow.
You didn't even try.

Grief made you angry,
and I understand that, too.
When your friend finally came,
your tears reproached him.
Honesty required it.

"If only---
if only you had been here."

You didn't come right out
and say it,
but you felt he had failed you.

Now, picking my way
through my own grief,
I shed honest tears.
I am angry with the God
who is my friend.

Show me, Martha.
Show all of us
what lies on the other side
of death and sorrow.

Stronger than sorrow,
more powerful than the smell of death.

Help us to see
Resurrection.

# I Don't Run Weddings

*On the third day there was a marriage at Cana in*
*Galilee, and the mother of Jesus was there; Jesus also*
*was invited to the marriage, with his disciples. When the*
*wine failed, the mother of Jesus said to him, "They have*
*no wine." And Jesus said to her, 'O woman, what have*
*you to do with me? My hour has not yet come." His*
*mother said to the servants, "Do whatever he tells you."*
*...Jesus said to them, "Fill the jars with water." And*
*they filled them up to the brim. He said to them, "Now*
*draw some out, and take it to the steward of the feast."*
*So they took it. When the steward of the feast tasted the*
*water, now become wine... John 2: 1–5, 7–9 a.*

I'm not pushy at weddings, Mary.
As a wedding guest
it's my job to order
goblets or salad forks
from the computer print–out
at the bridal registry.

It's my job
to walk down the aisle
on the arm of the young man
in the tuxedo,
to smile my way through a receiving line,
to leave the buffet table with chicken salad
and a sliver of cake.
I'm just a guest,
and that's fine with me.

I leave the fashionable details
to somebody else.
It's not my job
to run the wedding.

But at Cana, Mary,
the wine was giving out,
and you insisted on being helpful.
Some would use the word "pushy."

It wasn't your problem,
but you made it your problem.
Who asked you
to take inventory?

"Don't worry, " you said.
"My son is here.
I'm sure he can help."

One hundred percent mother,
one hundred percent proud.
What harm to show him off a little?

He hung back at first.
"I'm not ready yet, Mother."
But you wouldn't take "no"
for an answer.

He didn't want to disappoint you,
so he came up with a miracle.

I know the feeling, Mary.

When it comes to my kids,
I look for miracles.
If they can pull it off
it says something
about me.

It might not work out.
Motherly managers seem to be
an endangered species.

But for doting mothers
who won't take "no" for an answer,
is it wrong to hope
that a miracle could happen?

*And they came to Bethsaida. And some people brought*
*to him a blind man, and begged him to touch him. And*
*he took the blind man by the hand, and led him out of the*
*village; and when he had spit on his eyes and laid his*
*hands upon him, he asked him, "Do you see anything?"*
*And he looked up and said, "I see men; but they look like*
*trees walking." Then again he laid his hands upon his*
*eyes; and he looked intently and was restored, and saw*
*everything clearly. And he sent him away to his home,*
*saying, "Do not even enter the village." Mark 8: 22–24.*

*And they brought to him a man who was deaf and had an*
*impediment in his speech; and they besought him to lay*
*his hand upon him. And taking him aside from the*
*multitude privately, he put his fingers into his ears, and*
*he spat and touched his tongue; and looking up to*
*heaven, he sighed, and said to him, "Ephphatha." that*
*is, "be opened." And his ears were opened, his tongue*
*was released, and he spoke plainly. And he charged*
*them to tell no one, but the more he charged them, the*
*more zealously they proclaimed it." Mark 7: 31–36*

Was it like fog lifting,
blind man of Bethsaida?
His hands left your eyes,
and in the shadows
you saw men like trees walking.
Again, his touch,
and even the fog was gone.
Yes! This time, yes!

But the healer said,
"Don't tell.
Stay away
from the village."

And you, deaf man,
when he touched your ears
and your tongue,
When he commanded, "Be open,"
and your friends heard
words pouring forth,
how could you have kept silence,
orders or not?

There was a miracle story
that needed telling,
and you told it.
The story had to come out.
Never mind what the healer had said.

Why was it important to the healer,
blind man---deaf man?
Why anonymously?
Why not let the world know?
What about his image?
If he had said,
"Go and tell,"
it would have made sense.

But why the big "Shhh?"
What did it mean,
that "Shhh" of God?

In our world
"Shhh" is out of fashion.
We go public
with our kindliness,
arrange publicity,
invite cameras in.

Like everyone else,
I do kindnesses
for display purposes.

Then why turn bashful
when God touches my life
with a miracle of healing?

He unravels the tangle
of my indecision,
rescues me
from a furnace of pain,
and I hear no "Shhh" from him.
It's my own "Shhh"
that holds me back.

There are miracle stories
that need telling,
my own miracle stories.
I must go and tell.

# Widow, I Don't Understand You

*And a poor widow came, and put in two copper coins,
which makes a penny. And he called his disciples to
him, and said to them, "Truly, I say to you, this poor
widow has put in more than all those who are contribut-
ing to the treasury. For they all contributed out of their
abundance; but she out of her poverty has put in everything she had, her whole living." Mark 12: 42–44.*

I never even knew your name, Widow,
but I'm curious.
Why did you give those two coins,
(that mite) away?

They say it was all the money you had,
but still such a small amount.
Nobody could have been impressed.
Even 100 % didn't land you on the honor roll
of star contributors.

It's hard for me to understand that.
I'm not like you.

We try to protect ourselves.
Oh, we believe in giving,
but we're careful
not to overdo it.

The sticker on the door reads:
"We gave at the office."
We never forget the tax write–off.

Every year it gets harder
to give recklessly,
without counting the cost.

Your little gift was actually reckless,
wasn't it?
And, you know, in the Lord's eyes
I guess that's what made it
a big one.

# Matthew, I Think I Know

*And when the Pharisees saw this, they said to his disciples, "Why does your teacher eat with tax collectors and sinners?"   Matthew 9: 11.*

Matthew,
and all you other tax collectors,
I think I know
why you were never chosen
Men of the Year.

The April deadline is near,
and again this time
the tax collector is making
off with my money.

I see only that I'm working hard
and not getting ahead,
and it's hard to trace
exactly how that tax dollar
is being spent.

I think I can guess
why people got into the habit
of hating you, Matthew.
Yet, when you think about it,
they didn't have it so bad.

Burdened taxpayers, yes,
but at least
they didn't have to wrestle
with the long form.

# *Did Your Hand Tremble?*

*There came a woman of Samaria to draw water.  Jesus
said to her, "Give me a drink."  For his disciples had
gone away into the city to buy food.  The Samaritan
woman said to him, "How is it that you, a Jew, ask a
drink of me, a woman of Samaria?"  For Jews have no
dealings with Samaritans.  Jesus answered her, "If you
knew the gift of God, and who it is that is saying to you,
Give me a drink,' you would have asked him, and he
would give you living water."  ....Jesus said to her,
""Everyone who drinks of this water will thirst again,
but whoever drinks of the water that I shall give him will
never thirst; the water that I shall give him will become
in him a spring of water welling up to eternal life."
John 4:  7–10, 13 & 14.*

Did your hand tremble, Woman of Samaria,
as you handed him the dipper?

There was a risk, of course,
risk for both of you.
His Jewish rules said,
"Don't talk,
not with a woman,
not in public.
Don't talk with a Samaritan.
She is not one of ours."

Your Samaritan rules said,
"Not with a stranger,
not with a Jew.

Jews and Samaritans
do not share water jars."

Samaritan woman,
how could he know
about your husbands?
Have you thought of that?
How did he guess
about your history?

The whole town knew,
but how could he know,
this stranger in town?

He sensed your need
to be seen as person,
not as woman,
not as Samaritan---
as person.
He knew your need for the living water,
the fresh new life of God within you.

He confided his own need
for water from Jacob's well.
He asked you to serve it,
knowing your thirst, too,
your need to be needed.

First He handed you a mirror,
and you saw yourself,
then you passed Him the dipper
and you felt how good it was to be needed.

Woman of Samaria,
I sense your excitement
as you rushed into town.
I understand your confusion,
leaving your water jar behind.

The Living Water
wasn't just for you, was it?
You hurried to share the cup,
to bring it to the others.

He offers me living water, too,
Woman of Samaria.
He has known my past,
has seen me as person.
He has noticed my thirst,
held the dipper to my lips.

Do I pass the cup
eagerly
to someone else?

In my life,
is the Living Water a slow trickle,
or is it a splash of joy?

# Homecoming Party

*And the son said to him, "Father, I have sinned against*
*heaven and before you; I am no longer worthy to be*
*called your son." But the father said to his servants,*
*"Bring quickly the best robe, and put it on him; and put*
*a ring on his hand, and shoes on his feet; and bring the*
*fatted calf and kill it, and let us eat and make merry; for*
*this my son was dead, and is alive again; he was lost,*
*and is found." And they began to make merry.*
*Luke 15: 21–24.*

Father of the Prodigal,
Could we remember together?

Let's talk about your son,
but first could we talk
about my sons?

I remember each of them
stomping away in anger,
close by, yet off in some far country.

And when my sons crept back
from that far country
of defiance,
I never once threw a homecoming party.

There was no feast,
no hugs,
no explosion of joy.
Disapproval was my weapon;

silence, my stance;
coldness, my punishment.

But what of you
and your son?
Why the fatted calf?
Why the embrace, the gifts,
the call for celebration?

Permissive?
Indulging your wayward son?
Maybe.

Or was the party for you, too?

Were you celebrating your own second chance?
Did you rejoice
in one more shot
at parenthood?

# *Why, Judas?*

*When Judas, his betrayer, saw that he was condemned,*
*he repented and brought back the thirty pieces of silver*
*to the chief priests and the elders, saying, "I have sinned*
*in betraying innocent blood." They said, "What is that*
*to us? See to it yourself." And throwing down the pieces*
*of silver in the temple, he departed; and he went and*
*hanged himself. Matthew, 27: 3–5.*

You, Judas...
You there in the shadows...
Just one question and then I'll go.
I have to ask you,
"Why?"

I am appalled...
not that you betrayed,
not that your betrayal killed,
not even the enormity of the loss.

I am appalled less
by the ugliness of your crime
than the knowledge
that you did it
for a handful of change.

The tragedy was trivialized,
the strong leader felled
for pocket money.

You had followed the Master,
but following wasn't the way you had dreamed it,
was it, Judas?

Obsessed by your dream
of what it should be,
you couldn't accept
what it was.

But why am I here, Judas,
studying you?
Why do I stand with you?
What am I doing with Christ's betrayer
here in the shadows?

Is it fear, Judas?
Do I have an uneasy feeling
that I, too,
may have a Judas side?

# A Motel Room---My Babylon

*By the waters of Babylon,*
*there we sat down and wept,*
*when we remembered Zion.*
*On the willows there*
*we hung up our lyres.*
*For there our captors*
*required of us songs,*
*and our tormentors, mirth, saying,*
*"Sing us one of the songs of Zion!"*
*How shall we sing the Lord's song*
*in a foreign land?  Psalm 137:  1–4.*

Children of Israel,
tonight, alone in this motel room,
I understand you.
I understand those lyres hanging silent
on a Babylonian tree.

Babylon, less–than–home,
a gulf of loneliness
between you
and the God who hears music.
The isolation of exile
had stilled your song.

"How shall we sing the Lord's song
in a foreign land?" you cried.

Now in this motel room,
in this less–than–home

where prayers won't come,
I feel it, too.
In my little exile I ask,
"How shall I sing?
How shall I pray?"

This is no place to build an altar.
It's impersonal,
like last night's room
and the room of the night before.

The floral print bedspread,
the serviceable carpeting,
the unremarkable water color
in its narrow chrome frame.

In the desk drawer I have found
motel letterhead
and the Gideon Bible.

I've stripped the plastic wrap
from the drinking glass
and performed the ribbon–cutting ceremony
in the bathroom.

I've installed myself.
Like an explorer planting a flag,
I've taken possession.
For now, this is home,
or it should be.

But it's an unlikely place for prayer.
My family seems impossibly far away.
How can I pray for them?
How shall I sing the Lord's song
in this foreign land?

Children of Israel,
I know a Savior who is not far away.
His coming to earth
made altars everlastingly portable.

He was born in an outbuilding
of a public inn
where reservations were scarce.

As he grew away from his home town
he must have missed family,
must have remembered the warm safety
of the carpenter shop.

He understands loneliness.
Now he comes to me in my loneliness.

Children of Israel,
even here
I can set up an altar.
Even in this motel room,
I think I can pray.

## He Was Talking to Us

*"Do not lay up for yourselves treasures on earth, where
moth and rust consume and where thieves break in and
steal, but lay up for yourselves treasures in heaven,
where neither moths mor rust consumes and where
thieves do not break in and steal.  For where your
treasure is, there will your heart be also."
Matthew 6:  19–21.*

People on the hillside,
he spoke the words
in your presence,
but he was talking to us.
He was talking
about our treasures.

Storage space,
our perennial problem.
"We need more storage space,"

We squirrel away treasures.
Piling up possessions
has become big business.
Twelve pairs of shoes,
crystal platters,
silver spoons,
fishing gear.
Storage space...storage space...
srorage space.

Moth crystals
and rust–proof paint
don't change anything,
because moths and rust
were never the real issue.

It's about priorities.
We keep forgetting something.
We forget
that we're just passing through.
This arrangement
was never meant to be
permanent.

You people on the hillside
had a little better sense of that...
wandering shepherds,
footloose fishermen,
simple villagers.

Treasures? What treasures?
What possessions?
What do you mean, storage space?

Yet, even for you
his warning came,
"Lay up for yourselves
treasures in heaven."

# I Meant It As a Joke

*and plaiting a crown of thorns they put it on his head,
and put a reed in his right hand.  And kneeling before
him they mocked him, saying, "Hail, King of the Jews!"
Matthew 27:  29.*

Are you the one?
Are you the soldier
who made His crown of thorns?
I have to talk to you.

For you, it must have been
like what happened to me today,
only worse...a lot worse.

I think you'd understand
how I meant it.
It was supposed to be a joke,
a clever touch.

At today's meeting
Mona had asked for it.
She was just charging ahead
with decisions,
not bothering to wait for suggestions,
and that got to me.

Then I saw my opening.
I'd cut her down to size.
Everybody would laugh
and we could get back on track.

I broke in with my bright comment,
but it didn't work out.
There was a little scattered laughter,
but mostly it just got quiet in the room.

Mona looked surprised...
hurt, maybe.
and then somebody else stepped in
to change the subject.

I meant it as a joke,
but I guess it backfired.

Now, for some reason,
I'm thinking about you
(whatever your name was).

I've never been a Roman soldier,
or any kind of a soldier,
but I can imagine
what it must have been like
the day you made that crown.

It was your moment, wasn't it?
You had pulled it off.
Your crown of thorns
had done its work.
The man's claims
were being swept away
in a flood of laughter.

Then maybe you looked down
and saw blood,
and you knew
it wasn't the blood of that Galilean
at all.

You looked down,
and you saw
that your own fingers had been torn
by the crown of thorns.

# Hey you!---You With the Palm Branches!

*The next day a great crowd who had come to the feast heard that Jesus was coming to Jerusalem. So they took branches of palm trees and went out to meet him, crying, "Hosanna! Blessed is he who comes in the name of the Lord, even the King of Israel!" John 12: 12 & 13.*

Hey you!
You kids with your palm branches,
you groupies who showed up
when you heard about the parade,

Admit it,
you were never more
than celebrity chasers.

That Sunday
you were all hoarse
with hosannas,
but Monday was the morning after.

On Monday Jerusalem streets were littered
with scraps of palm leaves,
and you were off somewhere, looking for new excitement.

On Monday he found out
who his friends were.
Feelings alone
weren't good enough.
They still aren't.

Palm Sunday excitement
comes and goes.
Hosannas pass in and out of fashion,
and branches have a way of wilting.

Only loyalty and friendship
have staying power.
I hope I've learned that.

I must climb the hill.
He is my friend.

For the God who is my friend,
I must climb the hill
and follow to the Cross.

# He Shrugged You Off

*But Mary stood weeping outside the tomb, and as she
wept she stooped to look into the tomb. Jesus said to
her, "Woman, why are you weeping? Whom do you
seek?" Supposing him to be the gardener, she said to
him, "Sir, if you have carried him away, tell me where
you have laid him, and I will take him away." Jesus said
to her, "Mary." She turned and said to him in Hebrew
"Rabboni!" (which means Teacher). Jesus said to her,
"Do not hold me, for I have not yet ascended to the
Father..." John 20: 11, 15–17a.*

You clung to him,
Mary of Magdala,
and you wept.
You were not ashamed to feel.

Since seven demons had gone,
you had felt whole again,
and with this healer
you could be yourself.

"Do not hold me,"
he said,
beginning to walk away.

You can't keep anyone, Mary.
Our Lord wanted you to learn that.
He wants me to learn it, too.

"Do not hold me," he says
to everyone who clings
to yesterday's miracle.

You got used to it, Mary.
If we live, we have to get used to it.
Life is about saying good–bye.

Good–bye may be temporary,
but life is about
saying good–bye.

# And the Earth Shook

*And behold, the curtain of the temple was torn in two,*
*from top to bottom; and the earth shook, and the rocks*
*were split.  Matthew 27:  51.*

You who stood at the Cross,
tell me something.
When the ground trembled,
did you see it
as some sort of announcement?

In my childhood
when trains passed through our town,
the ground shook,
and we paid attention.

It meant something.
Sometimes an arrival,
sometimes departure,
but that shivering ground
carried some message.

For you at the Cross,
the message was "departure."
The gentle teacher hung dying,
and only a few had come to say good–bye.

You had no way of knowing
the real message was "arrival."

How could you have seen
that tragic leavetaking
as a beginning?
Easter's secret
was still hidden.

How could you have guessed
that the hate–built Cross
on that trembling hill
actually meant arrival...
the arrival of death–proof love?

# I Could Use Singing Lessons

*But about midnight Paul and Silas were praying and singing hymns to God, and the prisoners were listening to them, and suddenly there was a great earthquake, so that the foundations of the prison were shaken; and immediately all the doors were opened and everyone's fetters were unfastened. Acts 16: 25 & 26.*

Paul, I think I could use
some singing lessons.
Singing may be the only way
out of my prison.
It seemed to work for you.

You see, I feel trapped,
hemmed in by routine
and frustration
and petty worries.

I've always thought of myself
as your basic optimist.
If the fruit gets too ripe,
I bake banana bread.

But I feel trapped today.
Joy is somewhere out there
beyond the bars.

Maybe if you'd hum a few lines
I'd learn to sing again, Paul.
I could use some lessons.

# A Bird in the Rain

*He waited another seven days, and again he sent forth*
*the dove out of the ark; and the dove came back to him*
*in the evening, and lo, in her mouth a freshly plucked*
*olive leaf; so Noah knew that the waters had subsided*
*from the earth. Then he waited another seven days, and*
*sent forth the dove; and she did not return to him*
*anymore. Genesis 8: 10–12.*

A desperation move, wasn't it, Noah,
sending a bird
out into the rain?

It was your way of saying,
"Tell me it's clearing, Lord.
Put my world back in shape."

Your clumsy ark---
a vulnerable container
for the world's fresh start---
and you grew weary of that rain
drumming on the roof.

Keeping an eye on that whole menagerie
was no picnic.
Forty days in that pitching boat,
bobbing around and getting nowhere.

Forty days of smells
and bumping into each other in the dark.

How could you take
even one more day
of yelping and roaring
and sniffing and chirping?

For our world,
this feels like Day 40, Noah.
Waters have been rising too long,
sloshing against the side.

We're tired of picking our way
across a slippery deck,
tired of feeling adrift,
riding out the storm.

A rainbow would be nice,
but the important thing
is getting back to normal,
breaking out of the suffocating closeness,
stepping out on solid ground.

We open a window and wait.
Will a bird fly back through the mist,
a sprig of good new in its beak?

We could use one fluttering bird
to tell us it's over.

# Who? Me?--Words to a Rookie Prophet

*Then I said, "Ah, Lord God! Behold, I do not know how to speak, for I am only a youth." But the Lord said to me, "Do not say, 'I am only a youth'; for to all to whom I send you, you shall go, and whatever I command you, you shall speak. Be not afraid of them, for I am with you to deliver you, says the Lord." Then the Lord put forth his hand and touched my mouth; and the Lord said to me, "Behold, I have put my words in your mouth." Jeremiah 1: 6–9.*

"Don't ask me, Lord.
I can't handle it."

When God tapped you
on the shoulder, Jeremiah,
you were reluctant.
No, worse than that,
you were scared stiff.

God wanted to draw his people
back into unity.
He needed a spokesman,
and you were the one
he called out of line.

The role called
for a fearless prophet---
confident stride,
a voice like thunder,
a Superstar.

There you were, Jeremiah---
just a kid, a rookie,
tripping on your robes,
the crown of leadership
sliding down
over your eyes.

You didn't match the job description,
hadn't even applied
for the job.
All you could think to say was,
"Who?  Me?
I'm too young, Lord.
Look around.
I'm not cut out for this."

But God had made up his mind.
Somehow he convinced you.
"Don't worry, Jeremiah,
We'll make it fit."

It was you he sent
to the alterations department,
and not your prophet's crown.

"You don't feel big enough,"  God said.
"I'll make you big enough.
Go for it!"

We're not that different, Jeremiah.
When God calls us out of line,
we all try to duck.

"I'm too old."
"I'm too young."
"I'm too shy."
"Look how I've managed my life."

We all beg off.
"Your work needs doing,
I know that, Lord,
but why me?"

And God's answer
never changes.
"I'll make you big enough.
Go for it!"